This book belongs to:

Published by Ladybird Books Ltd
A Penguin Company
Penguin Books Ltd, 80 Strand, London WC2R 0RL, UK
Penguin Books Australia Ltd, Camberwell, Victoria, Australia
Penguin Books (NZ) Ltd, 67 Apollo Drive, Rosedale, North Shore 0632, New Zealand

1 3 5 7 9 10 8 6 4 2

ISBN 978-1-84646-523-9

Printed in Italy

Jungle
Animals

written by Geraldine Taylor
illustrated by David Kearney

Some hot regions of the
Earth have jungle
in them.

North
America

Europe

Africa

Equator

South
America

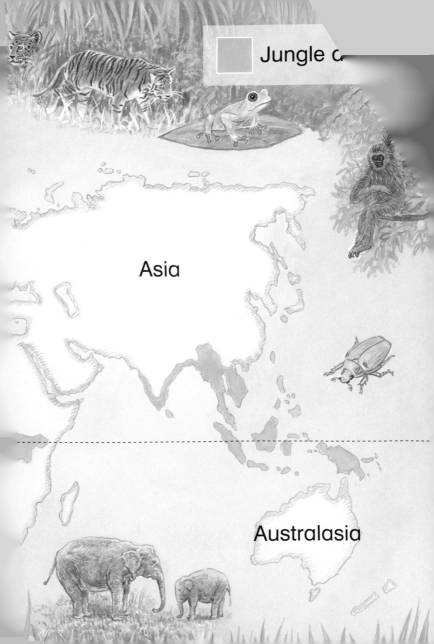

Jungle a

Asia

Australasia

The jungle has trees,
plants and water.
Many animals live there.

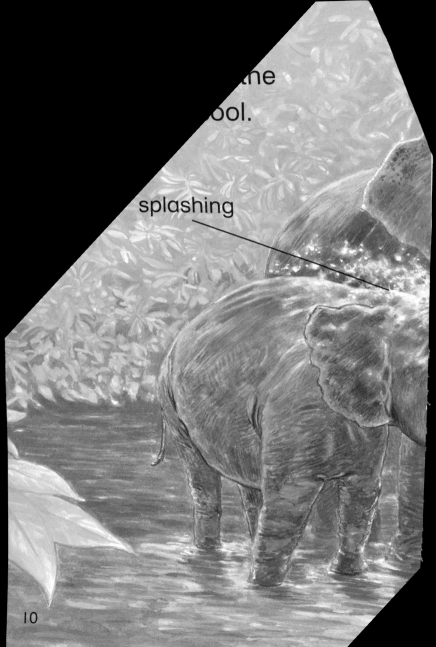

... the
...ol.

splashing

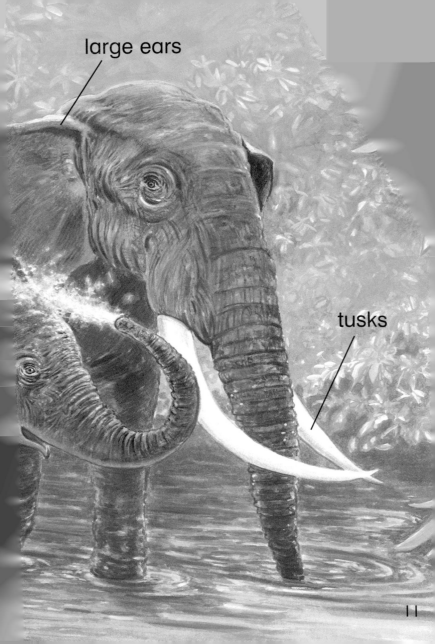

large ears

tusks

11

...codiles hide in the ...ater. They have long tails ...o help them swim.

scales

strong tail

eyes on top of head

13

Iguanas live in trees near the water. They eat plants.

scales

long tail

claws

Gorillas eat plants, too.
They sleep in the trees.

large
hands

nest

long arms

baby
gorilla

Cobras live in the jungle.
They can kill people.

body up to
five metres long

fangs

hood

eggs

19

Jaguars can hide in the trees. They can run fast and they can swim.

strong body

soft fur

large eyes

Tigers run fast, too.
They can hide in the plants.

strong claws

stripy pattern

long whiskers

Toucans live in the trees. They cannot fly very fast.

glossy black feathers

large bill for picking fruit

Howler monkeys live in the trees. You can hear them a long way away.

howling
mouth

strong tail

Which is your favourite animal?

Index